The Girl In The White Pinafore

by Jiggs Burgess

©2017: revised 2019

Jiggs Burgess

©2017 by Jiggs Burgess

All rights reserved.

Amateur and Stock production rights controlled exclusively by Jiggs Burgess, 3015 FM 1287, Graham, TX. No performance of the play may be given without obtaining in advanced written permission from Jiggs Burgess, payment obtained, and production scripts purchased. Please contact Jiggs Burgess @ jiggsb1@gmail.com for more information.

Thank you to--

The Girl In The White Pinafore

Betty and Bill Burgess, for not sending me away to the state home in Wichita Falls, even though it was mighty temping.

Brooks Aubrey Eastwood and Roberta Lackavage, without whom I'd never have discovered the story of New London.

Sarah Swatzell for encouraging me not to throw the whole dang thing in the trash.

Lori Penn Cox, Obelea Rue and the entire Olney Cub theatre department for a beautiful "scenes from" version for the 2018 UIL One Act Play contest. You will always be the first to inhabit these rolls and you did so with beauty and brilliance.

Ashlee Thigpen Howard. Thank you for all the hard work promoting me, even though I gave you such a hard time.

Diana Harvey for hanging in there and listening when I'm down. And whipping me into shape when I've been bad.

Ello Black for all that late night cheer-leading and because, you know, Ello Rules.

And to Jack and Diane Cody for always being there to "spur my donkey" when it needs spurring.

Above all I want to thank all the folks who continue to honor me by telling me their family's stories. The tragedy of the New London School explosion left scars across generations. Whether you or your audiences know it, the lives of those children continue to touch ours on a daily basis.

Be well. Break legs. Steal hearts.

Jiggs Burgess

Jiggs Burgess

For the victims and survivors of the New London School explosion, 03/18/1937.

The Girl In The White Pinafore

A one act cutting, or "scenes from", of The Girl In The White Pinafore was originally presented by Olney High School, Olney, TX and had it's first performance on February 26, 2018. The performance was directed by Lori Cox and Obelea Rue. The cast and crew were as follows:

CAST

Amelia Davis..Jae Montgomery
Mary Davis...Jenny Ford
John Davis..Hunter Simmons
William Chesley Shaw...Erik Cuba
Nadine Davis Williams/Chorus...............................Heidi Rodriguez
Lucy Everett.. LaAnna Golden
Lem Davis..Carter Hinson
E.W. Reagan/Chorus...Micheal Liming
Sam Shaw...Mason Spivey
Eli Cody/Chorus..Oscar Flores
Ethel Mayhew/Chorus.......................................Hayley Ondricek
Major Gaston Howard/Chorus....................Lance Sprague
Earl Clover...Wyatt Wilk
Chorus...Gilbert Acuna Jr.
Chorus..Ana Buzduga

CREW

Stage Manager...Baylee Bernhardt
Lighting..Melanie Allen
Sound... Gary Turner
Property Master..Andrea Ortiz
Costume Manager..Camryn Stone

ALTERNATES/UNDERSTUDIES

Kiara Allen, Saskia Baecker, Ryan Clayton, Fatima Marquez

THE GIRL IN THE WHITE PINAFORE

Cutting by Lori Cox, Obelea Rue, Jiggs Burgess

Jiggs Burgess

Characters

7M/5F/2M V.O.

RADIO ANNOUNCER (v.o. only)

*MAJOR HOWARD (v.o. or combination)

W.C. SHAW (M)-- superintendent of New London Schools

AMELIA DAVIS (F)-- the girl in the white pinafore; died in the New London explosion

CHILDREN'S CHORUS-- victims of the New London explosion

MARY DAVIS (F)-- Amelia's mother

JOHN DAVIS (M)-- Amelia's father

*NADINE DAVIS (F)-- Amelia's younger sister; a nurse

*LUCY EVERETT (F)-- a new nurse

LEM DAVIS (M)-- Amelia's brother

*E.W. REAGAN (M)-- president of the New London school board

SAM SHAW (M)-- W.C.'s son; often appears with Amelia, but remains silent

*ELI CODY (M)-- a victim of the explosion

*MR. BUTLER (M)-- wood shop teacher; flipped switch that sets off the explosion

*ETHEL MAYHEW (F)-- a victim of the explosion

*The CHILDREN'S CHORUS can play most of the minor roles with simple costume changes. AMELIA, MARY, W.C., and SAM may not be doubled. In this way, one could get away with 3f+3M and

chorus. At the very least, this allows for flexibility in cast breakdown and/or size.

**MARY DAVIS and W.C. SHAW may be played by two actors. Each actor would be billed as YOUNG MARY DAVIS or OLD MARY DAVIS, and YOUNG W.C. SHAW or OLD W.C. SHAW, according to his/her role.

Jiggs Burgess

SCENE-- APRIL 28, 1962/ MARCH 18,1937 COME GRACIOUS SPIRIT-- ONE ACT OPEN**

**See ALT OPENING for full open if desired. May require further cuts.

In easy view, are two (or more) radios which light at the appropriate times. One a 1930's style wooden radio, and the other an early 1960s model(plastic or chrome). There may be several of each style scattered across the stage. Both radios' dials begin to flicker as if they are trying to come on. In darkness we hear old time terrestrial radio static, then "tuning" noises. Voices start singing low "Come, Gracious Spirit, Heavenly Dove" as a ominous, red wash silhouettes bodies thrown by the explosion.

W.C. SHAW and MARY are rolled on in their wheelchairs on opposite sides of the stage by nurses. While MARY's chair mainly stays in place, on occasion WC SHAW's wheelchair is manipulated, controlled, rolled into place by the CHILDREN'S CHORUS. Static, tuning sounds--

We are aware of the sound of a heartbeat layered onto the sound. 1937 radio light comes up steady. Light comes up to silhouette AMELIA standing among the bodies.

RADIO ANNOUNCER: ...Mr. W.C. Shaw will be testifying before the military court of inquiry...

MAJOR HOWARD: *(On 1930s radio.) Please state your name.*

SHAW: William Chesley Shaw. W.C.

> *Tuning sounds/static as the broadcast fades out.*

AMELIA AND CHILDREN'S CHORUS: *(softly, separately and overlapping)* March 18, 1937... March 18, 1937... March 18, 1937...etc...

> *Gracious Spirit continues to play/be sung, but softly under. The heartbeat gets louder and faster as appropriate.*

RADIO ANNOUNCER: Folks, it's finally going to be sunny and warm out there. God is smiling on this, the 18th day of March, 1937. *(Radio fades under Amelia's line)*

AMELIA: On March 18, 1937...

> *The children's chorus speaks out of synch with each other--*

CHILDREN'S CHORUS: On March 18, 1937...

> *Until they come together.--*

AMELIA AND CHILDREN'S CHORUS: On March 18, 1937... I died.

> *The tuning sounds continue.*

MAJOR HOWARD: *(On 1930s radio)* You may speak freely, openly, and honestly. Do you understand, Mr Shaw? Mr. Shaw?

SHAW: I do...yes, sir.

> *The heartbeat stops suddenly. AMELIA looks confused, reaches out and collapses/is carried to her grave. Gracious Spirit swells then fades into...*

SCENE-- 1937 MARCH 18 JUST A DREAM

> *JOHN DAVIS has awakened with a start.*

Jiggs Burgess

MARY: John? Honey?

JOHN: *(startled)* Mary.

MARY: What's wrong? *(she rises and goes to him)*

JOHN: A bad dream is all. Go back to bed. It's still early.

MARY: What was it this time?

JOHN: Nothing...not really.

MARY: John.

JOHN: *(sighs)* There was a cliff. I was standing at the bottom with rocks and rubble everywhere, looking for Amelia and Lem. I could hear Amelia, she was singing an old hymn, but I couldn't find her...when I looked up, there were these birds, hundreds of them. The most beautiful things you ever saw...Beautiful and fragile and...Iridescent. Is that the word? You know, like oil on water. Beautiful, but dangerous, not natural...Then it was like they remembered they weren't supposed to fly and they started falling. One by one, but together at the sametime. Falling like... I...I don't know...rain isn't the right word. They came crashing down and there were so many of them. I was trying to catch them, to save even one. All the sudden they weren't birds anymore...they...they were...kids. And I knew every single one of them. I could call their names. I knew them but I couldn't save them. No matter how hard I tried, I couldn't...They fell and shattered right there at my feet. Broken. There was nothing I could do, Mary. Nothing.

MARY: John, you've been having those dreams ever since church on Sunday and I don't like it. It's a bad omen is what it is.

JOHN: Now Mary, you know I don't take no stock--

MARY: You remember what that revival preacher said? That there are prophets walking, John. Prophets big and small--

The Girl In The White Pinafore

JOHN: *(Lets out a sudden laugh.)* If God's gotten that far down the line, this old world's in a whole heap of trouble.

MARY: John!

JOHN: It wasn't anything but a bad dream. Go back to sleep. I've got to get to the buses.

MARY: I'd best go ahead and get breakfast on. Mildred and I are goin' into Tyler today to pick up the new radio. (pause) We're just so blessed, aren't we?

JOHN: (Pulls MARY close.) I was blessed the minute I met you.

MARY: You go on now. You've got a bus to drive and I have kids to feed. And we don't need any more surprises like Nadine. I'm too old for that.

JOHN: I love you, Maw.

MARY: Love you too, Paw. Now git.

JOHN exits, MARY begins to hum a hymn, returning to her wheelchair. The radio fades from 1930s to 1960s.

SCENE-- APRIL 28, 1962 TRAINING THE NEW GIRL

1960s radio flickers to life. A hymn is playing.

MAJOR HOWARD: *(from 1930s radio)* Mr. Shaw?

SHAW: Could you repeat the question?

MAJOR HOWARD: Did you see the testimony from Mr. Dowling?

SHAW: *(slightly confused)* I was... I was attending funeral services.

MAJOR HOWARD: Your son?

13

SHAW: Yes. Sam.

> *1930s radio flickers out. Two nurses, NADINE and LUCY, enter to attend him. NADINE is showing LUCY her duties on the first day of the job.*
>
> *NADINE and LUCY enter with an old rolling tray filled with medicines, water, pill cups, blood pressure cuffs, etc.*
>
> *NADINE is taking LUCY on her first day rounds. From here on out LUCY will come in periodically to check on SHAW, adjust his blanket, etc., almost as if they have a bond.*
>
> *NADINE will take SHAW'S blood pressure and temperature as LUCY records the numbers on SHAW'S charts, preps pills, makes sure SHAW takes the pills, and whatever other business can be found. There should be a casualness to this scene, at the same time a feel of studied perpetual motion. They are talking, as nurses often do, through the work, and through the patient.*

NADINE: Mr. Shaw? Let's turn this down, ok? Mr. Shaw, this is Nurse Everett. She's new and I'm going to be showing her how we do things around here.

> *Shaw is still mumbling names.*

LUCY: Pleased to meet you, Mr.--

> *SHAW grabs LUCY'S hand and looks at her as a child might look at his mother, eyes pleading for help. AMELIA steps up behind her, watching.*

The Girl In The White Pinafore

SHAW: Betty Lou, Emma, Phinas, Evan...

NADINE: Now, you let go of her hand,Mr. Shaw. (to Lucy) Don't you pay him no never mind. He's been gone from this world for sometime now.

AMELIA lightly touches LUCY'S shouder, LUCY. shudders.

LUCY: I swan, it's cold in here.

SHAW: *(sees AMELIA)* Sam...

LUCY goes about her work, checking SNAW's chart, prepping pills and whatnot. The following cnversation should take place in a "over the shoulder" kind of way. LUCY only half listening while working.

AMELIA sneaks down and unties LUCY's shoe laces.

LUCY: Who's that?

NADINE: Who's who?

LUCY: Sam.

NADINE: Some old ghost from his past is my guess. Folks live long enough and there'll be a ghost attached to 'em. Mostly memories. Things in their heads. Ghosts only they can see. Those don't bother me so much as the real ones that pop up from time to time.

LUCY: Uh-huh.

NADINE: I'll tell you one thing, though, If you ever come across a little girl in here in a blue dress and white pinafore and red hair ribbons, you just scoot right on by and come back later.

LUCY: Why?

NADINE: Because she's one of the real ones.

Jiggs Burgess

LUCY: *(laughs)* Right. Listen Nadine, I'm used to pranks on rookies--

NADINE: I'm not kidding. But you'll learn.

    LUCY notices her shoestring is untied, bends down to retie it.

SHAW: *(He's watched AMELIA)* Amelia! Don't be common.

NADINE: I don't remember her, but I had a sister named Amelia.

LUCY: How's that?

NADINE: What?

LUCY: How's that? That you don't remember your own sister.

NADINE: She died. In the school explosion? Back in, what, 1937? Horrible thing. Killed about 300 folks. Mostly kids. Mostly my sister's age.

LUCY: I've never heard of such a thing.

NADINE: Well folks around here don't talk about it much. There was a gas leak under the brand new school. Gas didn't have any smell to it back then.

LUCY: Really, I thought it smells like rotten eggs.

NADINE: No. They add that smell in, because of the New London School so people know if there's a leak.

LUCY: Well, I'll be. Learn something new everyday.

NADINE: Killed my sister and lots more besides. A lot of them are buried over there in the Pleasant Hill Cemetery. It plumb breaks your heart to go over their and see all those tombstones with the same date. March 18, 1937.

LUCY: I'll be. I never knew.

NADINE: My brother, Lem, he made it out alive, but he had all these scars. I think he always thought he should've gone with Amelia. Took to drink. Crashed his car. Such a shame. He was a sweet-hearted man. None of them would ever talk about it. either.

The Girl In The White Pinafore

LUCY: How sad.

NADINE: Then daddy died. Mamma, well, she just never lost faith, though. Never missed a lick of church until she had her stroke.

LUCY: God bless a strong woman.

NADINE: Amen to that. She'd go up to that graveyard, kneel beside Amelia's grave and and just about spend the day cryin', but she never said a word to me about Amelia or the explosion.

LUCY: Well, I'll be.

NADINE: Mr. Shaw, here, was the superintendent.

LUCY: You don't say?

NADINE: Lots of folks blamed him. There was even this rhyme. We'd jump rope or do one of the hand clappin' games to it.

LUCY: I used to love those games.

NADINE: How'd that go? Let's see--

CHILDREN'S CHORUS echoes NADINE as she recites.

Mary, Mary
Jack and Jill
How many children
Did it kill?

Mattie, Mattie
Sim and Will,
count the graves
upon the hill.

LUCY: That's kind of creepy.

SHAW: Stop it! Stop it, you hear me? Stop it right now. *(He grabs LUCY'S hand.)* Please. Tell them to stop.

LUCY: Nadine?

NADINE: Ok, Mr. Shaw. I'm sorry, I didn't mean to upset you.

Jiggs Burgess

LUCY: Maybe he thinks you're Amelia. Do you look like her?

NADINE: I don't know. Mamma never kept pictures. It must've been hard, Mr. Shaw takin' the blame all these years.

SHAW: I didn't do anything, I didn't.

LUCY: Yes, sir. I know, you just rest rest for now, Mr. Shaw.

SHAW calms at her touch.

NADINE: We need to move on.

LUCY: Mr. Shaw? Mr. Shaw, I'll be back to bring you your lunch, ok?

MAJOR HOWARD: (On 1930s radio) Mr. Shaw?

SHAW: I'm sorry...could you ask the question again?

MAJOR HOWARD: (on 1930s radio) Whose decision was it to switch from a boiler set up to gas heaters?

SHAW: It was mine, sir.

SCENE-- 1937 BREAKFAST

1930s radio lights. The Davis kitchen.
MARY is getting breakfast on the table.

LEM: Mornin' Mamma.

MARY: Mornin'. You feelin' better?

LEM: Yes 'm. Felt like my head was goin' to fall off yesterday, but I'm alright now.

MARY: Good. Where's that sister of yours?

LEM: Up there chattering away about Amelia Earhart to her dolls.

MARY: She's excited they have the same name. Sister! Sister, you get in here!

LEM: Well, she's about to drive me nuts--

AMELIA enters.

The Girl In The White Pinafore

MARY: Wel, good mornin' sunshine.

AMELIA: Mornin' mamma.

MARY: Why do you have on your Sunday dress?

LEM: She's trying to look good for that sissified bookworm, Sam Shaw.

AMELIA: I AM NOT!

LEM: You are too. I see how you get all googly eyed and giggly when he comes around.

AMELIA: I do not! Sam's just my friend.

LEM: You like him, but he's not interested in you. You're just a little girl.

AMELIA: You take that back--

MARY: Now Amelia.

AMELIA: I swear--

MARY: Amelia Rose Davis, we do not take oaths--

AMELIA: But Mamma--

MARY: I said that's enough. If Lem is wrong, you tell me why you'r so dressed up to go to school?

LEM: I'm gonna go finish up in the barn before the bus gets here. I'll come get you, squirt.

AMELIA: Don't call me squirt.

LEM: OK, L'il bit.

AMELIA: Maw--

MARY: Lem--

LEM: OK, OK. *(exits)*

Jiggs Burgess

MARY: Where did you get those awful hair ribbons? They're so...red.

AMELIA: I won 'em from Leslie playing jacks.

MARY: I see. Amelia, we do not take oaths or swear and we do not gamble in this house. You give those ribbons back.

AMELIA: I think they're pretty.

MARY: You give 'em back. Today. Now, you going to tell me why you're all dressed up, or am I going to have to get a switch?

AMELIA: Mamma... I just thought I'd look nice--

MARY: Out with it, what are you schemin'?

AMELIA: Well...I thought I'd look nice for the trip into town to pick up our new radio.

MARY: No ma'am. You have school.

AMELIA: But there ain't nothin' goin' on at school today. We always get out early on PTA days. Only we're not today and a lot of the teachers are gone anyway, so what are we going to do? Just sit there all day?

MARY: You're off tomorrow. Do you want me to wait? I'll have to find a ride into town if I do. I'm lucky Mildred has to go in today.

AMELIA: No! We have to have it today! Amelia Earhart is supposed to leave Hawaii today... It's so exciting and adventuresome. Just think about bein' out there in the blue yonder all by yourself in a big ole silver plane--

MARY: Well, you cannot miss school so you can sit home and listen to a radio. Good Lord. I don't know what children are coming to these days. Maybe we shouldn't even have a radio in the house at all.

AMELIA: But Mamma--

MARY: I said no, Amelia.

AMELIA: But Nadine gets to go. It's not fair.

MARY: Nadine is two years old, Amelia.

AMELIA: It's still not fair.

LEM: C'mon squirt, bus is here.

AMELIA: I said don't call me that!

LEM : Whoa, now--

MARY: *(sighs)* Go. Go on now. Both of you. But, Amelia...you get anything on that dress and I'll tan your hide. You got that?

AMELIA: *(sullen)* Yes, ma'am.

MARY: Now come on over here and give me a kiss, baby girl.

AMELIA: No! I hate you!

> *AMELIA runs out, sobbing.*

LEM: Amelia, you get back here! You should give her a good whoopin'--

MARY: I'll take care of it after school. Now scoot. Don't keep your daddy waiting.

> *LEM exits. MARY sighs, stares after them, returns to her wheelchair.*

MAJOR HOWARD: *(from 1930s radio)* Are you feeling alright, Mr. Shaw? Would you like to have a short recess? Maybe a drink of water?

SHAW: No, sir, please continue.

SCENE-- 1962 THE REQUEST

> *1960s radio lights up. A hymn is playing low. NADINE DAVIS WILLIAMS enters bringing MARY a tray of food.*

NADINE: Mamma?

> *MARY hums along to the song. Hum-*

Jiggs Burgess

> *ming might be a kind word for it. She grunts the rhythm and tune, but in her head she is leading the choir.*

NADINE: Mamma...It's time to eat a little somethin'... Mamma, you have to eat. If you don't eat, you're going to just fade away and that would make me so sad.

> *MARY stops her humming. She looks clearly and defiantly at NADINE.*

MARY: I want to go home.

NADINE: You are home, Mamma.

MARY: She needs help.

NADINE: Who, Mamma, who needs help?

> *MARY reaches out and pats NADINE softly on the cheek "hums" along with "Rock of Ages."*

MARY: My baby girl.

NADINE: *(Overcome)* Oh Mamma, I have...I have to go now. I'll come check on you before I leave for home, OK? *(kisses her and exits)*

> *MARY continues to sing. AMELIA crosses to MARY. MARY reaches for her, but it seems AMELIA can't quite bring herself to reach out to her mother.*

AMELIA: Mamma? I...I *(love you...)*

SHAW: ...could you ask the question again?

MAJOR HOWARD: *(on the 1930s radio)* Whose decision was it to switch from a boiler system?

SHAW: It was mine, sir.

The Girl In The White Pinafore

CHILDREN whisper. "I died."

MAJOR HOWARD: And no one else.

SHAW: No sir.

SCENE-- SPRING 1936 BUILD IT UP WITH GOLD AND SILVER

The 1930s radio lights up.

SHAW and E.W. REAGAN, the school board president, are walking the grounds of the new school, the kids play nearby.

E.W.: ...We out of money W.C.? Because last time I looked, money was rolling in. We're still the richest school in Texas...hell, maybe even the world.

SHAW: Now dang it E.W., I tell you there is just no need for such a frivolous--

E.W.: All Coach Carroll wants are some lights for the football field. It's 1937, W.C., not 1912, there's no need for us not to be up to date--

SHAW: E.W., nobody is going to come to a football game after dark! These people are farmers and roughnecks, E.W. The farmers go to bed as soon as the sun goes down, and the roughnecks go to the pool halls. It's a waste of money.

E.W.: It's a good idea, W.C.

SHAW: I think it's in bad taste to be spending so much on something so...frivolous. Especially with what everyone else in the country is going through right now. I just think we need save as much as we can for tough times. I want to make sure the kids that come after I'm gone are as well situated as my kids are now.

E.W.: We changed the heating set up, didn't we? And you're getting the gas changed over?

SHAW: Yes, but--

Jiggs Burgess

E.W.: And the new gas set up will save us even more. Enough money, I think, that we can do right by the kids with lights on the football field. Is that your boy? You already got him on the payroll, W.C.?

They stop to watch the children.

SHAW: Sam! Where's Mrs. Avery?

SAM: Jim Bob got hit in the nose with a ball and she went get him cleaned up. She asked me to look after her class.

E.W.: Taking care of a full class of kids already? I guess you're thinking about taking after your old man and going off to Sam Houston Normal? Become a teacher?

SAM: I guess so, sir.

SHAW: Now don't lie to the man, son. Tell him where you really want to go.

SAM: I'd like to go back East. To Harvard.

E.W.: *(whistles)* Harvard, you say? I'll be. W.C., looks like you got a Yankee on your hands here. Why not Sam Houston? Or the University of Texas? Plenty of fine folks went to UT.

SAM: Yes sir. It's just that...well, Harvard graduates presidents, and I'd like to be President someday.

E.W.: You don't say.

SAM: Yes, sir. Teddy Roosevelt went to Harvard.

E.W.: (snorts) Teddy Roosevelt. I see. Son, let me tell you somethin' that will serve you right well in both this life and the next: Harvard might graduate presidents, but UT graduates governors of Texas. And a governor of Texas beats the hell out of the President of the United States any day.

SAM: *(Embarrassed.)* Yes, sir. I'll remember that sir.

SHAW: You run along now.

SAM: Yes sir.

SCENE-- 1936 THE DOVE

E.W.: Good looking kid, W.C.

AMELIA: Sam! Sam, come here! Can you help him? *(holding a hurt dove.)*

SHAW: Smart as a whip too. He just might be Harvard material.

E.W.: Expensive. Did you strike oil in the basement of that house we built for you? If so, we're entitled to our cut. *(E.W. Exits, SHAW returns to wheelchair.)*

SAM: I don't know, Amelia, he seems to be hurt pretty bad.

AMELIA: What kind of bird is he?

SAM: A mourning dove.

AMELIA: *(pause)* My Mamma says that mourning doves are Godly creatures. That whenever you hear a dove, it's to remind you that the Holy Ghost is always with you.

SAM: That's what my mamma says too.

AMELIA: How do you know?

SAM: How do I know what?

AMELIA: How do you know it's a mourning dove?

SAM: Do you see these three black dots on his wing?

AMELIA: Uh-huh.

SAM: That's part of it. They're supposed to represent the Trinity. And this one, up near his eye?

AMELIA: Uh-huh.

SAM: Well, that one's supposed represent the tears Mary shed for Jesus. I suppose that's the mourning part of it. That and his call

Jiggs Burgess

sounds like he's sad.

AMELIA: Oh. I thought it was because we hear them in the morning.

SAM: *(he smiles)* That's a different kind of morning.

AMELIA: Little Tommy Avery said if he ever got himself a dove like that he'd fry him up and eat him.

SAM: He did did he?

AMELIA: Uh huh. You know what I told him? I told him that he could fry up any old squirrels he could get his hands on, but to leave them doves alone. He shouldn't be eatin' the Holy Ghost. That just ain't right.

SAM: No. No it's not.

AMELIA: *(pause)* Sam?

SAM: Uh huh?

AMELIA: Do you think girls can fly?

SAM: Now what kind of question is that?

AMELIA: Well, I said I wanted to fly airplanes when I grow up just like Amelia Earhart. You know she's going to try to fly around the world all by herself? And Edna said she wanted to be a farmer. And you know what Little Tommy said?

SAM: I can't imagine.

AMELIA: He said that girls weren't meant to do man stuff, and that I'd go to hell if I even tried. And that Edna could do what she wanted cause she was going to hell anyway on account she's an Episcopalian.

SAM: Don't you listen to Little Tommy. Like a lot of folks these days, he's misguided.

AMELIA: So you think girls can fly?

SAM: If you're talking about airplanes, I don't see why not. I suppose

The Girl In The White Pinafore

girls can do most anything they want.

AMELIA: Really?

SAM: (the dove) His wing's broken pretty badly, Amelia. Kindest thing we could do might be to just to put him down.

AMELIA: Sam, we've got to help him.

SAM: Amelia, sometimes it's better--

AMELIA: You have to, Sam. You HAVE to.

SAM: *(sighs)* I'll tell you what.

AMELIA: What?

SAM: If you'll help me take care of him, I'll see what I can do.

AMELIA: Do you think I can keep him? I mean after he gets better? For a pet.

SAM: Not if he can fly.

AMELIA: Awww.

SAM: Now, how would you like it if someone took you away from your home forever?

AMELIA: Mad, I guess.

SAM: But if he doesn't learn how to fly again--

AMELIA: I'll take the best care of him. I swear.

SAM: Good. Now let's go see what we can do for this little guy.

MAJOR HOWARD: *(On 1930s radio.)* Mr. Shaw, were you the man who gave the orders for the connection with the Parade Oil Company pipeline?

SHAW: I was partly responsible.

CHILDREN whisper.

MAJOR HOWARD: Partly?

SHAW: The end decision was mine, sir.

SCENE-- 1962 THE TRIALS OF LUCY

> *1937 fades. AMELIA stands at SHAW's side as LUCY enters.*

LUCY: Mr. Shaw I've got your dinner. It looks real--

> *LUCY suddenly sees Amelia.*

LUCY: *(Terrified)* Oh, Good Lord in Heaven!

> *LUCY runs out.*

SHAW: Go away. You're the devil.

AMELIA: I'm what you made me. You remember Willy? He wanted to be a soldier, didn't he, Mr. Shaw.

> *Underneath the folowing, the CHILDREN'S CHORUS whisper, what they dreamt they would be when they grow up.*

SHAW: Please, Amelia, please--

AMELIA: Sue and Ned--

SHAW: Sue wanted to grow up and have two boys and two girls. Ned.... poor Ned wanted to be a teacher like me...Sam--

> *AMELIA rejoins the CHILDREN"S CHORUS. LUCY and NADINE enter.*

LUCY: ...Right there. Right beside him.

NADINE: She's gone, Lucy. I tried to warn you. I told you to just come on back after a while. Mr. Shaw, you hungry? You must be, with folks runnin' out of here at every little disturbance--

LUCY: Now listen here, Nadine--

The Girl In The White Pinafore

NADINE: Oh, hush, I'm teasin' with you. I'm just happy you didn't drop the tray for me to come back and clean up.

LUCY: Well, I don't know...a job's a job and I've got bills to pay.

NADINE: Don't we all. Now Mr. Shaw, Miss Lucy here is going to stay and feed you. You just make your friend behave.

LUCY: Oh, Lord help me.

NADINE: I'm going to go check on Mamma.

LUCY: How's she doing?

NADINE: Her color's not good...her breathing...

LUCY: Oh, Nadine, I'm so sorry.

NADINE: I don't know, Lucy, maybe it would be better--

LUCY: You go on now, I'll handle things as best I can here.

MAJOR HOWARD: *(On 1930s radio.)* Mr. Shaw?

SHAW: *(slightly confused)* Yes?

MAJOR HOWARD: You were saying?

SHAW: I was... I was attending funeral services.

MAJOR HOWARD: *(coldly)* You have our deepest sympathies. We would like to find the cause of this tragedy so that no other parent has to bury their child in this manner.

SHAW: Yes sir.

SCENE 1937-- SOME BROTHERLY ADVICE

LEM: Hey, squirt.

AMELIA: I told you not to call me that!

LEM: Whoa, what's stuck in your craw?

AMELIA: Nothin'.

Jiggs Burgess

LEM: You still sore at Mamma?

AMELIA: It's not fair, Lemmy. I've been waiting all this time for that radio.

LEM: It don't matter if you think it's fair or not. She's your maw, and she's been a good one too.

AMELIA: I know, Lemmy. I just--

LEM: Let me ask you this, does she beat you?

AMELIA: No...but she threatens to sometimes.

LEM: Well, sometimes, I think she oughta.

AMELIA: Lem!

LEM: I'm just teasin' and you know it.

AMELIA: I know. I feel awful.

LEM: You should.

AMELIA: When I get home, I'm gonna give her a big kiss and tell her how sorry I am and I'll even wash the dishes.

LEM: You wash the dishes anyway.

AMELIA: I know, but tonight I won't complain. Lem?

LEM: Uh huh?

AMELIA: You think she hates me now?

LEM: Are you kidding? Knowin' her, she probably forgave you before you hit the door. Now go on, squirt.

AMELIA: Dang it, Lem. Don't call me squirt.

LEM: I love you, squirt.

AMELIA: I love you too, Lem.

LEM: Now, git L'il bit.

The Girl In The White Pinafore

MAJOR HOWARD: Were you the one who directed the janitor to make the connection from the waste line to the school?

> *CHILDREN whisper and become more agitated from here to the explosion.*

SHAW: Yes...yes, sir.

MAJOR HOWARD: Mr. Shaw? Mr. Shaw do you need a break? Mr. Shaw?

SCENE-- 1937 LOVE'S SACRIFICE

> *The 1937 radio glows softly, a report about Amelia Earhardt plays under the transition. A 6th grade classroom and the wood shop in the basement.*
>
> *AMELIA DAVIS, ETHEL MAYHEW, ELI CODY are in the classroom. LEM and MR. BUTLER are in the shop. The CHILDREN'S CHOURUS begins a low ticking sound at first, building to the explosion at the end of the scene. AMELIA fidgets with her hair ribbons. At the same time LEM is in the shop with MR. BUTLER. MR. BUTLER is humming "Gracious Spirit" and working on an electric sander. The scenes are played back and forth. The lines can be adjusted to make a natural feeling whole.*

ELI: *(whispering)* Amelia. Amelia, switch seats with me, would ya?

MR. BUTLER: Lem...hey, Lem! You awake?

AMELIA: Why? So you can set next to your girlfriend?

LEM: Uh...what?

ELI: Awww, Amelia. Come on--

ETHEL: Amelia Davis! He ain't my boyfriend. We just like to talk is

Jiggs Burgess

all.

MR. BUTLER: Hand me that screw driver, would you? You ok? You look like somthin' the cat drug in.

AMELIA: And hold hands--

ETHEL: Amelia!

LEM: I just don't feel good, Mr. Butler. Like my head is going to explode. Just like yesterday.

AMELIA: I saw y'all back behind the gym. Don't say I didn't--

ELI: Amelia, that just ain't true...completely.

MR. BUTLER: You too? Hand me that screw. I've just about got this fixed.

ETHEL: I had a splinter.

ELI: And besides, I could tell your Mamma that you've been smoochin' up on Bennett Connor. And I could tell Bennett that you've been smoochin' up on Sam Shaw.

AMELIA: That's a lie! You wouldn't!

ELI: Hide and watch.

LEM: You got a headache too?

MR. BUTLER: All day. You feel sick at your stomach?

LEM: A little. Mainly just tired and a headache.

MR. BUTLER: Must be something going around.

AMELIA: That's a lie and you know it, Eli Cody.

ELI: Did you have a splinter?

AMELIA: Eli Cody, I ain't never goin' to talk to you again. Ethel could you help me get these out?

ETHEL: Why are you takin' 'em out? They look pretty.

AMELIA: Mamma said I have to give them back.

The Girl In The White Pinafore

MR. BUTLER: I tell you what, the bell's about to ring, why don't you go on and get you some fresh air.

LEM: But, I'm not finished sanding my table.

MR. BUTLER: That'll keep. Go on, get out of here. See you Monday.

LEM: Yes, sir.

> *MR. BUTLER continues to hum and work. Looking at the sander and admiring his handy work.*

ELI: Awww, c'mon Amelia...the bell's about to ring anyway.

ETHEL: You really tied these in here.

AMELIA: You take it back about Bennett.

ELI: I take it back, you weren't smoochin on Bennett. Or Sam.

AMELIA: Well... OK, I guess.

> *Eli and AMELIA switch chairs. The ticking/stomping gets louder.*
>
> *MR. BUTLER makes his way to an electrical outlet, plugs in the sander, and flips the switch. A crackling sound and a drum booms or stomping from the kids. The radios flicker and the lights dim. There is, at first, just a small flicker of a spark that seems to hang in the air for a moment and then catch.*

ELI: I had my fingers crossed.

AMELIA: Eli Cody, you're a horrible human being and I ain't ever going to talk to you ever again.

ELI: Promise--?

SCENE-- 1937 THE EXPLOSION

Jiggs Burgess

Explosion.

The explosion happens in three sections, expanding from the shop area then across the acting area.

At first all lights go black, coming up with smoke on the shop only. There is a slow muffled heartbeat. Mr. Butler is seen being blown back, reaching fo rward in slow motion. Blackout.

In blackout a cacophony of explosive sound.

Light flows back up from bottom to top on shop area and center, showing the children center stage being blown back in slow motion. Again the sound of a slow muffled heartbeat.

In blackout a cacophony of explosive sound.

Blackout. Light flows back up from bottom to top across all acting areas, all being blown away. The sound of the heart beat, then silence, then static.

Then a ringing like a ringing in the ears which mutates into shouts and alarms. This again evolves into static and radio
sounds that becomes...

JOHN: *(calling)* Lem? Amelia? Amelia?

RADIO ANNOUNCER: ...ladies and gentlemen, please...has anyone seen Amelia Davis...she was last seen wearing a white pinafore and red hair ribbons...please let the Davis family know if anyone has seen

The Girl In The White Pinafore

Amelia...

> *LEM finds AMRLIA, carries her to JOHN and MARY.*

MARY: No!

> *During the following, bodies are "discovered," recovered, and carried, slowly to their burial plot.*

SCENE-- 1937 THE INQUIRY

RADIO ANNOUNCER: ...Ladies and gentlemen, Mr. W.C. Shaw has just been called to testify before the military court of inquiry on his roll in the explosion at the New London School. Major Gaston Howard will be asking the questions.

> *The inquiry bounces from the 1937 inquiry into the explosion to flashbacks of mistakes made. MAJOR HOWARD can be on stage at this point.*

MAJOR HOWARD: Please state your name for the record.

SHAW: William Chesley Shaw.

MAJOR HOWARD: What is your occupation?

SHAW: Superintendent for the New London Consolidated School District.

MAJOR HOWARD: This is a court of inquiry not one of a criminal nature. Do you understand?

SHAW: I do, sir.

MAJOR HOWARD: We have heard testimony from a Mr. J.L. Downing, the initial architect for the school. Were you present for Mr. Dowing's testimony?

SHAW: No, sir. I was at my...my...*(trails off)*

MAJOR HOWARD: Your son, Mr. Shaw?

SHAW: My son's funeral, yes sir. Please forgive me.

MAJOR HOWARD: *(coldly)* You have our deepest sympathies. We would like to find the cause of this tragedy so that no other parent has to bury their child in this manner. Mr. Downing testified that, in his plans, he had called for heating the school with a boiler type system. Is this correct?

SHAW: Yes sir.

MAJOR HOWARD: However, his plans for a boiler system were not implemented. Can you tell us why that is?

SHAW: To save money.

MAJOR HOWARD: And whose decision was it to switch to gas heaters?

> *Flashback. E.W. REAGAN,*
> *president of the school board*
> *and WC SHAW.*

E.W.: ...I think I speak for the whole of the board when I say we think it's a good idea, W.C.

SHAW: Mr. Reagan, are we sure the quality--

E.W.: Mr. Belew assures us that his Gas-Steam brand radiators are of the highest quality and, here's the part I think you'll like most W.C., we won't have to make any changes to the design. It'll be cheaper to install and cheaper to run.

SHAW: What about venting? I need to talk to Mr. Downing. Won't we have to vent these radiators?

E.W.: That's the beauty, W.C., Mr. Belew says we don't have to vent them.

SHAW: Well, let's take it to the board, then. See what they think.

The Girl In The White Pinafore

E.W.: No need. We all know you're looking for ways to cut costs, W.C.... All you need to do is call Mr. Belew. You have the authorization to sign the contracts--

MAJOR HOWARD: Mr. Shaw?

SHAW: It was mine, sir.

MAJOR HOWARD: Who provides the gas contracts for the New London school district?

SHAW: United Gas. Until recently.

MAJOR HOWARD: How recently?

SHAW: Almost a month.

MAJOR HOWARD: And after that?

SHAW: We tapped into Parade Oil's waste line.

MAJOR HOWARD: Into what is referred to as green or wet gas?

SHAW: Yes sir.

MAJOR HOWARD: Mr. Shaw, were you the man who gave the orders for the connection with the Parade Oil Company pipeline?

Flashback.

E.W.: ...W.C., we don't see why we can't just tap into the waste line that runs next to the school.

SHAW: Those are Parade Oil lines. I'll pay a visit to Mr. Clover at Parade Oil to get the permission. I'm sure it won't be a problem, and it will certainly save us money.

E.W.: Permission? Hell, W.C., do you know anybody who isn't tapped into a waste line somewhere? Nobody's going to miss it.

SHAW: I just think--

E.W.: That's a problem, you thinking too much.

SHAW: Just let me talk with the men over at Parade--

MAJOR HOWARD: Mr. Shaw? Mr Shaw, would you like me to repeat the question?

SHAW: The decision was mine, sir.

MAJOR HOWARD: Did you discuss this at anytime in an official capacity in front of the school board?

SHAW: Not with the school board as a whole. No, sir.

MAJOR HOWARD: Did you seek permission from Parade Oil to use their waste pipe as a source of free gas?

SHAW: Yes, sir.

MAJOR HOWARD: This was Mr. Earl Clover, was it?

SHAW: Yes, sir.

MAJOR HOWARD: Do you know whether Mr. Clover has returned, yet, from his son's funeral?

SHAW: *(shaken)* No, sir. I do not.

MAJOR HOWARD: Were you the one who directed the janitor to make the connection?

E.W.: *(flashback)* WC, just get a line run to the school and tie in under the basement. You've got someone on staff that could do that for you. Maybe that janitor who did the water lines out back.

SHAW: *(breaking down)* Yes...yes, sir. It was my decision sir...

MAJOR HOWARD: Mr. Shaw? Mr. Shaw do you need a break? Mr. Shaw?

> *WC returns to his wheelchair.*
> *Gracious Spirit plays on the*
> *1930s radio.*

SCENE 1937-- A FEW DAYS LATER

JOHN: Mary? Come to bed. Mary--

MARY: I should've let her go with me, John...she would've been here

The Girl In The White Pinafore

with me. All she wanted--

JOHN: Mary.

MARY: "I hate you..." Oh, God, John, I can't stand this pain. *(JOHN goes to her)* Don't. Don't touch me.

JOHN: Mary--...They had no bones.

> *JOHN looks at her, stops, and exhales. It seems as if all his will has left him. He will tell his story this one time, but never speak of the explosion again.*

MARY: Oh, God!

> *JOHN looks at his bandaged hands.*

JOHN: I waded through the glass and the concrete, the buckets of rubble, everything shattered...and then a body. They had been shattered from the inside out. Like they had no bones. They were...gelatin...Mary, they no longer held form. I knew every one of those kids, but I couldn't tell who it was I was carrying. Only that none of them were Amelia...So I had hope...for a time, I had hope...And then I heard your cries... I heard you scream... There was nothing I could do, Mary, there IS nothing I can do. God help me, there's nothing...but to close my eyes and try to forget... Can we just turn off the lights?

MARY: Don't you dare, John. Don't you dare turn out that light because if you do, it'll be tomorrow--

JOHN: Mary--

MARY: And if it gets to be tomorrow I don't know what I'm going to do because tomorrow's one more day away from Amelia. If there's tomorrow, then there's going to be one after that, and another, and another. *(pause)* Pray with me, John. John?

JOHN: I'm sorry. I can't, Mary. I just can't. Tomorrow's gonna come whether we sleep or not. Whether we pray or not. All we

Jiggs Burgess

can do is get through. Together. There's no prayer that'll help us, Mary. We have to go on with no help from God. Lem needs us. Nadine needs us--

MARY: I'll pray for the both of us, then.

JOHN: I'm sorry I just can't Mary. I'm just not that strong.

SCENE-- 1962 PERMISSION

MAJOR HOWARD: *(On 1930s radio)* Whose responsibility was it, Mr. Shaw?

SHAW: The end decision was mine, sir.

> *1962 radio is lit. Nadine is at her mother's side. MARY is breathing shallowly. LUCY enters. AMELIA watches the following--*

LUCY: How're you doing?

NADINE: About as well as can be expected, I suppose. She was holding this.

> *NADINE hands LUCY an old worn picture.*

I don't know where it came from.

LUCY: *(gasps)* Nadine...Nadine, this is the little girl.

NADINE: Read the back.

LUCY: Oh my Lord in heaven. This is your sister. Nadine...

NADINE: I've never seen that before. How'd she keep that from me?

LUCY: Oh, Nadine. Is there anything I can do for you?

NADINE: No. I'll be fine. You go on home now.

LUCY: Well...you let me know if there's anything I can do. I mean that, you hear?

The Girl In The White Pinafore

NADINE: I will.

> *LUCY exits. MARY is trying to sing, but her breathing will not allow her to. AMELIA is standing near, watching, wanting to reach out, but unable.*

NADINE: Mamma, don't try to sing, you hear? Please? Just breathe...If you need to go, you go. You hear, now? You go be with Daddy and Lem. And you go find Amelia, OK? She's probably been needing you pretty bad all these years.

MARY: *(with much effort-- is she talking to NADINE, or AMELIA?)* I love you, baby girl.

> *NADINE holds MARY'S hand as MARY takes a few shallow breaths and then exhales...*

NADINE: I love you, Mamma.

> *NADINE kisses MARY on the forehead. MARY is gone. AMELIA has been watching and begins "Old Man Shaw" sloftly, sadly...*

SCENE-- 1962 CONFRONTATION

MAJOR HOWARD: *(on 1930s radio)* Whose decision was it?

SHAW: It was mine, sir.

MAJOR HOWARD: And no one else.

SHAW: No sir. It was mine alone.

> *1962 radio glows.*

AMELIA: *(softly at first...confused and sad...)* Just how many died?

SHAW: Amelia.

AMELIA: How many died, Mr. Shaw?

Jiggs Burgess

SHAW: Understand, Amelia, I didn't know.

AMELIA: Understand? You're asking me to understand?

MARY: Calling from off. Amelia?

SHAW: I didn't know, Amelia. I wanted to do right. I wanted to save money.

AMELIA: At what cost?

> *SAM steps forward. The CHILDREN'S CHORUS step forward.*

SHAW: My children.

AMELIA: You mean Sam. You grieve Sam, but not the rest of us.

SHAW: That's not true. All these years--

AMELIA: How much were we worth, Mr. Shaw? What did our future cost?

SHAW: I loved all of you.

AMELIA: How much were we worth?

SHAW: Sam, tell her. Tell her how you went without sometimes--

SAM: It's time, dad.

SHAW: I don't--

AMELIA: How much did you save? How much were we worth?

SHAW: Amelia, please--

> *SHAW's breathing becomes ragged, labored.*

AMELIA: How many? How many mothers, fathers, writers, painters, farmers, soldiers? Do you know?

SHAW: Almost three hundred.

AMELIA: Three hundred regrets. I wanted to fly, and I wanted...I needed to tell her...I didn't have a chance. I didn't. Mamma never knew I was sorry--

MARY: *(Calling. O.S.)* Amelia?

SHAW: ...two hundred ninety four. Amelia--

AMELIA: How much were we worth Mr. Shaw? How much did you save?

SHAW: $250.84. Amelia, I can't breath.

AMELIA: Neither can I, Mr. Shaw... I couldn't... I couldn't tell Mamma I was sorry...For $250.84. (she does the math) Eighty five cents?...I was worth eighty five cents? All of us... eighty five cents each.

SHAW: Eighty five cents? Surely that's not right, Amelia, that can't be right...

AMELIA: It's what we were worth to you, Mr. Shaw.

SHAW: Eighty five cents? Oh, God help me. God help me.

W.C. Reaches for SAM.

SHAW: Sam... Sam, help me. Tell her Sam. Tell her--

AMELIA AND CHILDREN'S CHORUS: March 18, 1937...March, 18 1937...March 18, 1937..etc.

SAM: Amelia, that's enough. (to W.C.) You took the blame.

AMELIA: But Sam--

SAM: Amelia. It's time.

SHAW: Sam. Sam I can't breath...Help me Sam.

AMELIA: Eighty five cents, Sam. And the last thing I told Mamma was, "I hate you." Now, she's gone--

SAM: He already took the blame, Amelia. (to SHAW) You took the blame.

SHAW: It was my fault.

SAM: Not alone. There were others. Why? Why did you take the blame?

SHAW: Everyone had lost so much. My children. So many...Oh, Lord, forgive me.

> *Voices begin to sing. The song carries through to curtain.*

SAM: Dad, listen...It's time to go. Let's go home.

SHAW: No. I can't. First tell me that you forgive--

MARY: (off) Amelia?

SAM: It's not mine to forgive, dad...Ask yourself for forgiveness. Ask from those who still feel the pain.

SHAW: Amelia? I'm so sorry...please.

SAM: Dad?

SHAW: Sam, help me. I can't breath...Sam?

SAM: It's time to go home...Everyone's waiting.

SHAW: Not yet, Sam. Please, let me catch my breath a moment. Let me rest.

> *SAM begins to exit, but turns to watch AMELIA, who is unsure what she needs to do next. She is now lost in a way that she has never felt...AMELIA now stands among the CHILDREN'S CHORUS who...*

SCENE-- FINDING HOME

> *...form a back drop, an army of watchers for WC.*

MARY: *(calling, running in, a mother once again)* Amelia...Amelia?

AMELIA: Mamma?

The Girl In The White Pinafore

Amelia starts to run to MARY, but stops just short.

MARY: Amelia, come on, now, it's time to go home. Daddy's waiting, and Lem. And so many others. Let's go now.

AMELIA: I can't, Mamma...I'm afraid.

MARY: Afraid of what, Amelia? Everyone's been waiting for you for such a long time. Come along.

AMELIA: But, Mamma, I don't know how.

MARY: How to do what, sweetie?

AMELIA: Leave. I'm afraid.

MARY: Amelia, baby, I'll show you. I know the way. It's time. Let's go now.

SAM crosses to AMELIA, carrying the dove from before. Amelia is in both time periods at once. SAM and AMELIA stroke the dove and make ready to release him.

SAM: Amelia... it's time.

AMELIA: But Sam--

SAM: You promised, Amelia. Remember? You said when it was time,
we'd let him go. (Is SAM talking about the dove, or W.C.?)
That he could fly away home.

AMELIA: Sam, but what if it's not healed?

SAM: You have to have faith Amelia. Here. Take him. You let him go.

AMELIA: I can't.

SAM: You can. Go ahead. (to dove) Go, gracious spirit...(softly, to Amelia) Go gracious spirit...

AMELIA hesitates, unsure, and gently

45

Jiggs Burgess

> *lets the dove go.*

MARY: Amelia?

SAM: It's time go home Amelia, I hear your Mamma calling.

> *SAM turns back to watch the arc of the little dove as it wings its way home.*

AMELIA: Mamma?

MARY: Amelia.

AMELIA: I'm so sorry, Mamma.

MARY: For what, L'il bit?

AMELIA: I didn't mean what I said. I didn't mean it, Mamma.

MARY: Oh, Amelia. I know.

AMELIA: You don't hate me?

MARY: Oh, Amelia, no. Come on, baby girl. Let's go home.

AMELIA: I've been gone so long, Mamma.

MARY: I know, L'il Bit. We've all been lost so long.

AMELIA: I didn't get to...My life, Mamma. My life it meant nothing.

MARY: It meant so much, Amelia. You don't know, do you?

AMELIA: Know what?

MARY: Your life saved so many others. With out you, so many other people would have died. You have to let go, Amelia.

> *AMELIA turns, tentatively at first, and runs into MARY'S deep embrace.*

AMELIA: I love you, Mamma.

MARY: I know. I love you too,

> *MARY and AMELIA join LEM and JOHN.*

The Girl In The White Pinafore

W.C. is alone, staring vacantly into the dark. The CHILDREN'S CHORUS and their families stand guard behind him, in the gray dimness. In their graves.

A glowing light comes up on W.C. He rises slowly from his wheelchair, reaching out to the light. The CHORUS looks up and out to where WC is reaching. A red ribbon falls from W.C.'s hand.

"Gracious Spirit, Heav'nly Dove" builds and fades as the lights swell to blinding levels, flicker, then blackout...

END OF PLAY

Jiggs Burgess

NOTES:

The CHILDREN'S CHORUS is to be used as the director sees fit to emphasize action, plot, theme, or transitions. They may repeat what's been said. They may create.They may also be used to manipulate SHAW into position on stage. No special permission is needed for this. However, the director may NOT give them new lines that are not a repeat of something said before or written for them by the author. Ex: CHORUS members may whisper/mumble, "On March 18, 1937, I died." They may NOT suddenly have an monologue about their life.

Sam - 8th grade
Amelia - 6th grade
MS grade 5-9
1937

sephia palette w/ red ribbons

THE GIRL IN THE
WHITE PINAFORE

Cutting for Denison HS by: Amy Jordan, Nikki Silva, Matthew Schielack

DKS - blacklight vintage costumes, pale makeup, neutral white/gray pale pastel

blue dress (1937)
white pinnefore
red hair ribbons

1930s/40s Texas ~ accents
★ Major Howard added

Jiggs Burgess

A one act cutting, or "scenes from", of The Girl In The White Pinafore was originally presented by Denison High School in Denison, TX and had it's first performance on February 2019. The performance was directed by Amy Jordan and Nikki Silva. Technical direction provided by Matthew Schielack. The cast and crew were as follows:

CAST

Amelia Davis	Canaan Thomas
Mary Davis	Albany Martin
John Davis	Jaden Petty
William Chesley Shaw	Donovan Garza
Nadine Davis Williams	Liz San Millan
Lucy Everett	Madison Broadway
Lem Davis	David Chick
Sam Shaw	Emily Carney
Eli Cody	Avery Martin
Ethel Mayhew/Chorus	Sydney Gardner
Young Nadine/Chorus	Avery Encalade
Chorus	Gracie Gardener
Chorus	Tate Mobley
Chorus	Skippy Levacy

CREW

Stage Manager	Mercedes Reed
Lighting	Isabelle Sawyer
Sound	Hunter Arban
Specials	Ethan Eubank
Projections	Faith Parum

ALTERNATES/UNDERSTUDIES

Paul McDaris, Hope Rhodes, Cadie Bates, Anthony Springborg, Patrick Schaufer

The Girl In The White Pinafore

L/S* — In darkness. There is a sudden explosion of almost unbearable sound and light.

Set: Lights come up dimly and we see US the mangled remains of the New London School. Busted concrete, protruding rebar, piles of brick, broken glass. We can make out the arches of where the glass widows were and above, partial lettering that reads... New London SchooL.

prop/set: Just down stage of the broken facade, a line of tombstones in a "v" formation. These are the tombstones of the child victims of the New London School explosion. The tombstones are large enough for the CHILDREN'S CHORUS to disappear behind and/or stand on from time to time. At the point of the "v" is AMELIA DAVIS'S tombstone. SAM SHAW'S is L of AMELIA. Each tombstone has the name and birth-date "chiseled" into it...different birth-dates, different epitaphs, but the same death-date: MARCH 18, 1937.

set/prop: DS right is a wheelchair and an old iron bed. This is MARY DAVIS'S home in 1937 and nursing home room in 1962.

DL is a wheelchair and a smalltabl with a radio appropriate for 1962. This is W.C. SHAW'S 1962 nursing-home room. He will from time to time tune through the radio static to calm the children's voices which torment him always.

A voice rings out in the gloom. And sings "Come Gracious Spirit, Heavenly Dove" throughout the following.

VOICE: Come, gracious spirit, heav'nly dove,
with light and comfort from above;
be thou our guardian, thou our guide;
o'er every thought and word preside,
O'er every thought and word preside...

S = Song for reference

MARY DAVIS and W.C. SHAW enter from opposite sides of the stage. MARY with the help of a cane, as she is her 1962 self. SHAW enters as the 1937 SHAW. Both come DS almost center, turn to make there way to their "home" space and we watch Mary as she transform into her 1937 self, while SHAW transforms into his 1962 self.

Chorus rises from behind their tombstones as a silent, loving scene happens between MARY and JOHN DR and NADINE helps SHAW into his chair, draping a shawl or blanket over his legs and exiting, leaving SHAW by himself DL. As the song fades, the children begin to speak, vacantly, out. At first one by one, then, repeating themselves, overlapping until the voices are so intermingled that they are unintelligible--

AMELIA: I wanted to fly.

CHILDREN'S CHORUS 1: I was going to teach.

CHILDREN'S CHORUS 2: I wanted to be a mother and a wife.

The Girl In The White Pinafore

CHILDREN'S CHORUS 3: I was going to work the land.

CHILDREN'S CHORUS 4: I dreamed of being a doctor.

CHILDREN'S CHORUS 5: I wanted to be a writer.

SAM SHAW: I wanted to be just like my dad.

> *They repeat, until...*

CHILDREN'S CHORUS: *(As one voice.)* On March 18, 1937 at 3:17 P.M... I died.

> *In unison, the CHILDREN'S CHORUS train their eyes on SHAW. AMELIA and SAM come of their tombstones and make their way to SHAW.*

CHILDREN'S CHORUS : *(softly at first)*
Mary, Mary
Jack and Jill
How many children
Did it kill?

SCENE 1962--

> *SHAW reaches out to SAM.*

SHAW: Sam? Sam. Talk to me...You turn around and talk to me.... Please, Sam. Amelia, why won't he speak?

AMELIA: He's lost his head, I'm afraid. You did that you know.

SHAW: It's you, you hateful little girl. You won't let him speak, will you? Sam? Sam! You speak to me.

AMELIA: Mary, Mary
Jack and Jill
How many souls
Did it still?

> *AMELIA shoots SAM a look, SAM collapses suddenly.*

SHAW: Amelia...Amelia...please.

AMELIA: Please, what Mr. Shaw?

SHAW: Wake him up.

AMELIA: But he's sleeping so peacefully right now. Hard to tell he's even breathing, isn't it?

SHAW: You hateful thing. You devil.

AMELIA: I am what you made me.

SHAW: Please, Amelia, let me talk to him. Just once. To tell him--

AMELIA: Tell him what, Mr. Shaw?

SHAW: That it wasn't my fault.

AMELIA: So sorry, Mr. Shaw, wrong answer.

> *Radio static. Tuning noises. The RADIO ANNOUNCER abruptly comes on mid sentence.*

RADIO ANNOUNCER: Has anyone seen Amelia Davis? She was wearing a blue dress and white pinafore and red hair ribbons. Please let the Davis family know if anyone has seen Amelia...

> *Radio fades to a low buzz.*

NIGTMARE SEQUENCE-- 1937

> *CHILDREN'S CHORUS, includin AMELIA, sing. AMELIA makes her was DS as JOHN watches the CHORUS, unable to understand who or what they are. As he is focused on the CHILDREN'S CHORUS, they slowly pull long red silks from under their collars, and drop them gently to the floor.*
>
> *JOHN turns and sees AMELIA, goes to*

The Girl In The White Pinafore

her. They turn to each other, mirror each other as they put their palms out, but do not touch. AMELIA turns away, singing, pulling a red silk from her neckline. JOHN returns to bed as the CHILDREN'S CHORUS fade out, leaving AMELIA singing the last few notes alone. She drops her silk.

JOHN awakens with a quick intake of air, looks around disoriented, and leaves the bed to look out at the early morning darkness. This awakens MARY.

MARY: John? What's wrong?

JOHN: A bad dream.

MARY: Another one? What was it this time?

JOHN: Nothin'.

MARY: John.

JOHN: I was looking for Amelia. I could hear her singing this old hymn like my mamma used to sing. When I looked up, there were these birds. They shimmered iridescent against the sun. All of the sudden, they started falling from the sky and shattering on the rocks below. But they weren't birds when they fell. They were kids. Falling, shattering right there at my feet.

MARY: I don't like these dreams, John. They worry me.

JOHN: Smiles, shaking it off. It was just a dream. (*JOHN turns and kisses her sweetly.*) Nothin' but a silly old dream. Now, you get back to bed, I've got to the buses.

JOHN exits as MARY transforms into Old Mary, humming "Rock of Ages."

<u>1962--SHAW</u>

> *Static and tuning noises come up as SHAW fumbles with the dial from his wheelchair. He is mumbling to himself, listing the names of the victims. He is in the throes of dementia.*

SHAW: Amelia, you just run along home, you hear? Boyd, Evelyn, Fae, Myrtle, Lillian, George, Betty, Ruth, etc. *(continues through out the scene)*

> *NADINE and LUCY enter with an old rolling tray filled with medicines, water, pill cups, blood pressure cuffs, etc.*
>
> *NADINE is taking LUCY on her first day rounds. From here on out LUCY will come in periodically to check on SHAW, adjust his blanket, etc., almost as if they have a bond.*
>
> *NADINE will take SHAW'S blood pressure and temperature as LUCY records the numbers on SHAW'S charts, preps pills, makes sure SHAW takes the pills, and whatever other business can be found. There should be a casualness to this scene, at the same time a feel of studied perpetual motion. They are talking, as nurses often do, through the work, and through the patient.*

NADINE: Mr. Shaw? Let's turn this down, ok? Mr. Shaw, this is Nurse Everett. I'm going to be showing her how we do things around here.

> *Shaw is still mumbling names.*

LUCY: Pleased to meet you, Mr.--

> *SHAW grabs LUCY'S hand and looks at her as a child might look at his mother,*

The Girl In The White Pinafore

> *eyes pleading for help. AMELIA steps up behind her, watching.*

SHAW: Betty Lou, Emma, Phinas, Evan...

NADINE: Now, you let go of her hand, Mr. Shaw. (to Lucy) Don't you pay him no never mind. He's been gone from this world for sometime now. *(AMELIA lightly touches LUCY'S shoulder, LUCY shudders.)*

LUCY: I swan, it's cold in here.

SHAW: *(sees AMELIA)* Sam...

> *LUCY goes about her work, checking SHAW's chart, prepping pills and whatnot. The following cnversation should take place in a "over the shoulder" kind of way. LUCY only half listening while working.*
>
> *AMELIA sneaks down and unties LUCY's shoe lace.*

LUCY: Who's that?

NADINE: Who's who?

LUCY: Sam.

NADINE: Some old ghost from his past is my guess. Folks live long enough and there'll be a ghost attached to 'em. Mostly memories. Things in their heads. Ghosts only they can see. Those don't bother me so much as the real ones that pop up from time to time.

LUCY: Uh-huh.

NADINE: I'll tell you one thing, though, If you ever come across a little girl in here in a blue dress and white pinafore and red hair ribbons, you just scoot right on by and come back Later.

LUCY: Why?

NADINE: Because she's one of the real ones.

Jiggs Burgess

LUCY: (laughs) Right. Listen Nadine, I might be new here, but I'm no rookie--

NADINE: I'm not kidding. But you'll learn.

> *LUCY notices her shoestring is untied, bends down to retie it.*

SHAW: *(He's watched AMELIA)* Amelia! Don't be common.

NADINE: I don't remember her, but I had a sister named Amelia.

LUCY: How's that?

NADINE: What?

LUCY: How's that? That you don't remember your own sister.

NADINE: She died. In the school explosion? Back in, what, 1937? Horrible thing. Killed about 300 folks. Mostly kids. Mostly my sister's age.

LUCY: I've never heard of such a thing.

NADINE: Well folks around here don't talk about it much. There was a gas leak under the brand new school. Gas didn't have any smell to it back then.

LUCY: Really, I thought it smells like rotten eggs.

NADINE: No. They add that smell in, because of the New London School. So people know if there's a leak.

LUCY: Well, I'll be. Learn something new everyday.

NADINE: Killed my sister and lots more besides. A lot of them are buried over there in the Pleasant Hill Cemetery. It plumb breaks your heart to go over their and see all those tombstones with the same date. March 18, 1937.

LUCY: I'll be. I never knew.

NADINE: My brother, Lem, he made it out alive, but he had all these scars. I think he always thought he should've gone with Amelia. Took to drink. Crashed his car. Such a shame. He was a sweet-

The Girl In The White Pinafore

hearted man. None of them would ever talk about it. either.

LUCY: How sad.

NADINE: Then daddy died. Mamma, well, she just never lost faith though. Never missed a lick of church until she had her stroke.

LUCY: God bless a strong woman.

NADINE: Amen to that. She'd go up to that graveyard, kneel beside Amelia's grave and and just about spend the day cryin', but she never said a word to me about Amelia or the explosion.

LUCY: Well, I'll be.

NADINE: Mr. Shaw, here, was the superintendent.

LUCY: You don't say?

NADINE: Lots of folks blamed him. There was even this rhyme. We'd jump rope or do one of the hand clappin' games to it.

LUCY: I used to love those games.

NADINE: How'd that go? Let's see--

> *CHILDREN'S CHORUS echoes NADINE as she recites.*

Mary, Mary
Jack and Jill
How many children
Did it kill?

Mattie, Mattie
Sim and Will,
count the graves
upon the hill.

LUCY: That's kind of creepy.

SHAW: Stop it! Stop it, you hear me? Stop it right now. *(He grabs LUCY'S hand.)* Please. Tell then to stop.

LUCY: Nadine?

NADINE: Ok, Mr. Shaw. I'm sorry, I didn't mean to upset you.

LUCY: Maybe he thinks you're Amelia. Do you look like her?

NADINE: I don't know. Mamma never kept pictures. It must've been hard, on old Mr. Shaw, here. Takin' the blame all these years.

SHAW: I didn't do anything, I didn't.

LUCY: Yes, sir. I know, you just rest rest for now, Mr. Shaw.

> *SHAW calms at her touch.*

NADINE: We need to move on.

LUCY: Mr. Shaw? Mr. Shaw, I'll be back to bring you your lunch, ok?

> *LUCY and NADINE exit. SHAW adjusts the radio. Static and tuning noises. MARY transitions to her younger self. She's making the bed, folding things, etc.*

SCENE-- 1932

LEM: Mornin' mamma.

MARY: Mornin'. Where's that sister of yours?

LEM: Up there singin' one of her song. Between that and the new radio comin' she's about to drive me nuts.

MARY: Now, Lem, have some grace. Well, there she is. Good mornin' sunshine. And just why do we have on our Sunday dress?

LEM: She's trying to look good for that sissified city boy book worm, Sam Shaw.

AMELIA: I AM NOT!

LEM: You are too. I see how you get all googly eyed and giggly when he comes around.

AMELIA: You take that back! You take that back right now, Lem, or I'll punch you, I swear--

The Girl In The White Pinafore

A fight ensues. AMELIA rushes at LEM. LEM calmly keeps her at bay with his hand on AMELIA'S head as she keeps swinging. MARY steps in, pulling AMELIA away. LEM taunts AMELIA. AMELIA responds. MARY steps between the two. This should be a lot of fun. Typical brother/sister.

MARY: Now Amelia, that's enough! Lem, you too.

LEM: I'm goin' to finish up ou in the barm before the bus gets here. I'll come get you when I hear it squirt.

AMELIA: Don't call me squirt!

LEM: OK, L'il Bit.

AMELIA: Maw-

MARY: Lem!

LEM: OK, OK. (exits)

MARY: Now, are you going to tell me why you're in your Sunday clothes, or am I going to have to get a switch?

AMELIA: I just thought I'd look nice.

MARY: For?

AMELIA: Well...I thout I'd look nice for the trip into town to pick up our new radio.

MARY: No ma'am.

AMELIA: Bur why?

MARY: You have school.

AMELIA: But mamma-

MARY: No.

AMELIA: Please?! Amelia Earhardt is supposed to leave Hawaii

61

today
and--

MARY: I said no, Amelia. And I mean it. You cannot miss school so you can sit home and listen to a radio. What are you thinking, child?

AMELIA: But--

MARY: Now you march yourself back to your room and change into your regular clothes.

LEM: C'mon, squirt. Bus is here.

MARY: (sighs) Go on. But if you get anything on that dress and I'll give your hide a tanning you won't soon forget. You got that?

AMELIA: Yes, ma'am.

MARY: Now, little girl, come give me a kiss.

AMELIA: NO! I HATE YOU! *(she rushes out, to her tombstone)*

LEM: AMELIA! *(he chases after her, exiting)*

MARY: That child's going to be the death of me.

SCENE 1962--

> *MARY begins to sing "ROCK OF AGES" as she transitions back into OLD MARY. Her words becoming garbled. AMELIA turns, watches, sings along with MARY. NADINE enters with a tray. AMELIA watches the whole scene from the edges.*
>
> *At the same time, LUCY enters and gently readjusts SHAW'S blanket, give him a drink of water, makes sure he's comfortable, and exits.*

NADINE: Mamma? Mamma, I brought you some food.

> *MARY is hum/singing ROCK OF AGES with*

The Girl In The White Pinafore

> *some difficulty.*

Yes, mamma, I know. Can you sing the words?

> *NADINE begins to sing the words, trying her best to get MARY to sing along.*

Rock of ages, cleft for me. Can you sing, mamma? Let me hide myself in thee. *(sighs)* You hungry, mamma? I brought you some food. Just a little? Oh please mamma, you have to eat. If you don't you're going to just fade away and that would make me so sad.

MARY: *(with difficulty)* I want to go home.

NADINE: You are home, Mamma.

MARY: I want to go home.

NADINE: This is where you live now.

MARY: She needs me. I'll take her home with me.

NADINE: Who, mamma, who needs you?

> *MARY reaches out and gently pats NADINE on the cheek.*

MARY: My little girl.

NADINE: *(overwhelmed)* I...I have to go, ok mamma? I..I'll check on you before I go home. I love you mamma.

> *MARY continues to sing/hum ROCK OF AGES. AMELIA reaches out to MARY, but can't touch her.*

AMELIA: I love you mamma...

<u>1932--THE DOVE</u>

> *Static, tuning noises. SAM moves forward. SHAW reaches for him. AMELIA*

Jiggs Burgess

> *comes rushing to SAM, pantomiming holding a dove.* Prop

SHAW: Sam...Sam!

AMELIA: Sam! Sam! Look!

SAM: Well look at that.

AMELIA: It's hurt. Can you help him?

SAM: I don't know. *(examines the bird)* He's hurt pretty bad.

AMELIA: What kind of bird is he?

SAM: A mourning dove.

AMELIA: That's what I thought. My mamma says that whenever you hear a dove, it's to remind you that the Holy Ghost is always with you...Sam?

SAM: Uh huh?

AMELIA: Do you think girls can fly?

SAM: Now what kind of question is that?

AMELIA: Well... I said that I wanted to fly airplanes when I grew up, just like Amelia Earhart. You know what Little Tommy Avery said?

SAM: I can't imgaine.

AMELIA: Well he said that girls weren't meant to do boy stuff and that I'd go to hell if I even tried.

SAM: Don't you listen to Little Tommy, he's got some peculiar notions.

AMELIA: So you think a girl can fly?

SAM: I suppose a girl can do about anything a boy can.

> *AMELIA gives SAM and excited hug, realizes what she is doing and turns*

The Girl In The White Pinafore

away, embarrassed.

AMELIA: Oh...Do you think I can keep him?

SAM: Not if he can fly.

AMELIA: Awww.

SAM: Don't you think he has a home to go back to?

AMELIA: I guess.

SAM: How would you like if someone took you away from your home forever?

AMELIA: But--

SAM: If we can fix him up, he needs to fly away home.

AMELIA: I guess.

SAM: So promise.

AMELIA: Promise what?

SAM: That when the time comes, we'll let him go.

> *Two ways to do this-- If SAM is played as AMELIA'S age, SAM spits in his palm and holds it out and waits for AMELIA to do the same. If SAM is played older, AMELIA spits in her palm and holds out her hand first, and waits for SAM to follow through.*

Good. Now, let's go see what we can do for this little guy.

> *Static, tuning noises.*

1962--LUNCH TIME

> *LUCY enters carrying SHAW'S lunch tray. The CHILDREN'S CHORUS gathers behind AMELIA and they move*

65

Jiggs Burgess

> *as one toward LUCY. They are almost playful. LUCY can see AMELIA.*

LUCY: Mr. Shaw, I've got your food. It looks real--

CHILDREN'S CHORUS: Lucy, Lucy
>Jack and Jill
>How many children
>Did it kill?

>Lucy, Lucy
>Sim and Will
>Count the graves
>upon the hill.

> *LUCY sees AMELIA. Terrified, she drops the tray and lets out a small scream, turns and runs out yelling--*

LUCY: Nadine! Nadine! Somebody help! There's a ghost! It's real!

SHAW: Go away.

AMELIA: Hey, Mr. Shaw.

SHAW: Don't be common, Amelia.

AMELIA: Oh, Mr. Shaw, you're going to hurt my feelings. I looked up to you, you know. Willy, Willy--

SHAW: Go away, you're the devil.

AMELIA: I am what you made me. Willy wanted to be a soldier, didn't he?

SHAW: A soldier, yes.

AMELIA: Sue and Ned--

SHAW: Sue wanted to grow up to be a mother. Ned...poor Ned. He wanted to be a teacher.

AMELIA: Willy, Willy

The Girl In The White Pinafore

SHAW: Please don't--

AMELIA: Sue and Ned--

SHAW: Amelia...please--

AMELIA: Heard his baby
    Lost his head.

SHAW: Oh, Lord, please help me.

AMELIA: Was it worth it, Mr. Shaw? All that money you saved?

SHAW: I didn't know. I didn't know! There was a flaw. In the design. Please, please, I didn't know.

> *AMELIA circles around as so not to be seen by LUCY and NADINE as they enter.*

LUCY: Right here! She was right here!

NADINE: She's gone Lucy. I tried to warn you.

LUCY: She called my name, Nadine. She called my name!

NADINE: Well, she must like you.

LUCY: You shut your mouth right up!

NADINE: *(picking up tray)* She's not here now. I'll come back with you
later and we'll see if we can't get him to eat.

1932-- GOOD INTENTIONS

> *Static, tuning sounds. Lunchtime. The children are playing, LEM crosses to AMELIA, she pushes past him, stil angry from the morning.*

LEM: Whoa there, Nellie. What you got stuck in your craw?

AMELIA: Nothin'.

LEM: You're still sore at mamma.

AMELIA: What of it?

LEM: If she don't give you a whoopin' for the way you acted, then maybe I should.

AMELIA: It's not fair, Lemmy.

LEM: It don't matter if you think it's fair or not. She's our maw, and she's a good one too. She don't ever really whip us.

AMELIA: She threatens to.

LEM: I think it'd break her heart to actually do it, though.

AMELIA: *(sighs)* I know. I just feel awful.

LEM: You should.

AMELIA: Well, when I get home, I'm going to give her a big hug and kiss, and I'm going to tell her how much I really love her. AND, I'm going to do the dishes tonight!

LEM: You do the dishes anyway.

AMELIA: Yeah. But tonight I won't complain. You just hide and watch.

A bell rings.

LEM: Well, that's somethin' I suppose. Now git along, Squirt.

AMELIA: Dang it Lem! Don't call me Squirt.

> *They share a secret handshake and a hug.*

LEM: I love you, Squirt.

AMELIA: I love you too, Lemmy.

LEM: Now git, L'il Bit.

> *LEM exits off. Static, tuning noises. AMELIA to the "classroom." an area*

The Girl In The White Pinafore

just around the tombstones. The CHILDREN CHORUS interact, listening and reacting.

A note. The explosion comes suddenly, as it would have in real life. The director may wish to subtly foreshadow it with a droning sound, but it should still come as a shock to the audience.

ELI: Amelia. Switch seats with me, would ya?

AMELIA: Why? So you can sit next to your girlfriend?

ELI: Awww, Amelia. Come on--

ETHEL: Amelia Davis! He ain't my boyfriend. We just like to talk is all--

AMELIA: And hold hands--

ETHEL: Amelia!

AMELIA: I saw y'all behind the gym. Don't say I didn't.

ELI: Now that ain't true...sort of.

ETHEL: I had a splinter.

ELI: And besides, you've been smoochin' up on Sam Shaw.

AMELIA: You're a liar! I ought to punch you square in the nose. Sam and I are good friends. We're taking care of a sick dove until it can fly. Ethel could you help me get these out?

ETHEL: Why are you taking them out? I think they look pretty.

AMELIA: Mamma says I have to give 'em back to Leslie.

ELI: C'mon, Amelia. The bell's about to ring anyway.

AMELIA: Take it back.

ELI: I take it back. You weren't smoochin' on Sam.

AMELIA: Well, OK...I guess.

Jiggs Burgess

> *ELI and AMELIA switch seats.*

ELI: I had my fingers crossed.

AMELIA: Eli Cody! You are a horrible human being and I'm never going to talk to you again.

ELI: Promise--

1937-- EXPLOSION

> *Staging this, of course, is up to the director or choreographer.*
>
> *There is sudden slow motion confusion and a chaos of sound, light, movement. This should be a horrible vision of poetry, beauty, and violence ending in a moment of complete and utter silence to allow us to take in the bodies strewn across the stage. Then a ringing and a in-rush of activity and static/tuning sounds as families look for their children.*

RADIO ANNOUNCER: ...has anyone seen Amelia Davis? She was wearing a blue dress with a white pinafore and red hair ribbons. Please let the Davis family know if anyone has seen Amelia.

> *LEM, JOHN, and MARY search and call for AMELIA, who is draped over her tombstone. MARY is the one who finds, screams and weeps, and takes the red-ribbons from AMELIA'S hand.*
>
> *Simultaneously, SHAW searches and calls through the devastation for SAM, who he eventually finds near SAM'S tombstone.*

MARY: AMELIA! NO! No, no, no, no, no, no....

The Girl In The White Pinafore

SHAW: SAM!

> *JOHN and LEM make their way to MARY and gently pull her away. MARY allows her self to be pulled away while clinging to one red ribbon.*
>
> *SHAW stumbles DS and LUCY comes to escort SHAW back to his wheelchair.*

SCENE 1937-- GRIEVING

MARY: I should've let her go, John. All she wanted was...I should've let her go with me...

JOHN: Now Mary, you can't--

MARY: All she wanted was one day, John...one day off and she'd still be here with me. All she wanted--

JOHN: Mary...

MARY: I want to scream, John. I want to scream. But who do I scream at? You? God? The ground at our feet? The dirt that covers her?

JOHN: Mary--

MARY: Who do I blame, John?

> *MARY shoots JOHN a look. He stops, exhales. It seems all his will has left him. This is the last time he will ever speak about the explosion again.*

JOHN: I don't know Mary. I don't know. I don't know why. I don't who to blame. Because I can't survive, Mary, if I thought God existed to do this to us...

They were there, just like the dream. All these children, these beautiful creatures, shattered at my feet. And there was nothing I could do...I just want to close my eyes and pretend that it didn't happen, to let it all fall away.

> *MARY reaches out to JOHN.*

MARY: Pray with me John.

> *JOHN turns away from her.*

JOHN: I'm sorry, Mary. I just can't.

MARY: John.

JOHN: Let's not, Mary. Let's not pray. Let's let it rest. It just hurts to talk about it. It wont do us any good.

MARY: Please, John, pray with me.

JOHN: You pray for me too, because I'm lost, Mary. I love you, but I don't know if I can ever fall on my knees again, Mary. So you pray for me too. Pray that God can forgive me for blaming him and just maybe I can find my own way.

> *JOHN exits. Static/tuning noises. As JOHN exits, MARY transforms into OLD MARY on her death bed, holding an old photo of AMELIA and her hair ribbons.*

1962-- MARY GOES HOME

> *NADINE attends MARY. Strokes her hair, sings to her, etc. NADINE finds and takes the photo from MARY. LUCY enters.*

LUCY: How's she doing?

NADINE: Not so good.

LUCY: How're you doing?

NADINE: About as well as can be expected, I suppose. She was holding this. I don't know where it came from. *[prop: picture]*

LUCY: Nadine....Oh...Nadine this is the little girl I saw.

The Girl In The White Pinafore

NADINE: That's my sister. I've never seen it before. How did she keep
that from me all these years?

LUCY: Oh, Nadine. Is there anything I can do for you?

NADINE: No. I'll be fine.

LUCY: Well, you let me know if there's anything I can do, you hear?

NADINE: I will.

> *LUCY exits. MARY is trying to to sing, but her breathing will not allow her to. AMELIA is standing near, watching, wanting to reach out, but unable.*

Mamma...It you need to go, you go. You hear now? You go be with Daddy and Lem. And you go find Amelia. OK? She's probably been needing you all these years. You just go on if you need to.

> *MARY nods her head and slowly reaches for NADINE'S face, bringing it close and kissing her on the forehead. the CHILDREN'S CHORUS begin to sing the line--*
>
> *"Do you hear a deathly knell?" Over and over. Softly at first.*

MARY: I love you little girl.

> *NADINE holds MARY'S hand and sings "Rock Of Ages" (counterpointing the CHILDREN'S CHORUS) as MARY takes a few shallow breaths and then exhales. AMELIA picks up and finishes "Rock Of Ages" as NADINE fades out.*
>
> *The CHILDREN'S CHORUS surround*

> *MARY, welcoming MARY in death to their world.*
>
> *AMELIA turns to SHAW, grief stricken and angry. Determined more than ever, now, to extract the answers she needs from SHAW.*

AMELIA: Just how many did it kill?

SHAW: Amelia

AMELIA: How many did it kill, Mr, Shaw?

SHAW: Understand, Amelia, I didn't know. Please. I didn't know.

AMELIA: Understand? You're asking me to understand?

SHAW: I didn't know, Amelia, I wanted to do right.

AMELIA: At what cost?

SHAW: Please, Amelia.

AMELIA: At what cost Mr. Shaw?

SHAW: My children.

AMELIA: You mean Sam. You greive Sam but not the rest of us.

SHAW: That's not true. All these years--

AMELIA: We had dreams too. How much were they worth, Mr. Shaw? What did our future cost you?

SHAW: I loved all of you.

AMELIA: At what cost did we die?

SHAW: I don't--

AMELIA: How much did you save? How much were we worth?

SHAW: Amelia, please--

AMELIA: Mary, Mary
    Jack and Jill

The Girl In The White Pinafore

> How many children
> Did it kill?

SHAW: Please--

AMELIA: Mattie, Mattie
> Sim and Will
> Count the graves
> Upon the hill--

Count the graves, Mr. Shaw. How many? How many mothers, fathers, writers, painters, farmers, soldiers? Do you know? I wanted to fly, and I wanted to...I didn't have a chance. I didn't. Mamma never knew I was sorry--

MARY: *(Calling, OS)* Amelia?

AMELIA: How much were we worth Mr. Shaw? How much did you save?

SHAW: $250.84. Amelia, I can't breath.

AMELIA: Neither can I, Mr. Shaw...I couldn't... For $250.84? *(she does the math)* Eighty five cents? I was worth eighty five cents? All of us Eighty five cents each.

> *SAM steps into the scene. From here on out, he'll start to take over.*

SHAW: Eighty five cents? Oh, God, help me. Help me. Sam. I can't breath. Help me. Tell her. Tell her how much--

AMELIA: Mary Mary
> Jack and Jill
> How many children
> Did it kill?

SAM: Amelia. That's enough.

AMELIA: But Sam--

SAM: That's enough, Amelia. Can't you see? He took the blame. *(to WC)* You took the blame.

AMELIA: Sam--

SAM: Amelia. It's time.

AMELIA: Eighty five cents, Sam. And the last thing I told Mamma was I hate you.

SAM: He took the blame. It's time. It's time to go home. Why, dad?

SHAW: It was my fault. I made the decisions.

SAM: Not alone. Why, dad? Why did you take all the blame?

> *VOICES begin to sing, carrying through to curtain.* backstage mic

SHAW: Everyone lost so much. My children. Oh Lord in Heaven, please forgive me. Amelia, forgive me.

> *W.C. Turns to AMELIA. AMELIA hesitates, and seems to accept his repentance, but she at a loss now. Her anger is what has held her to this world and she's not sure how to let it go.*

SHAW: I thought I was doing right. I'm so sorry...please. Sam. Help me, I can't breath. Sam?

> *SAM is watching AMELIA, who is now lost in a way she's never felt.*

SCENE-- 1962/1937 FINDING HOME

> *MARY enters, calling, searching, now a mother again.*
>
> *During the following, LUCY comes to check on SHAW. SHAW grabs LUCY'S hand. LUCY comforts him, he dies and LUCY gently rolls him off. This should not distract from the scene.*

The Girl In The White Pinafore

MARY: Amelia? Amelia...?

AMELIA: Mamma?

> *AMELIA starts to run to MARY, but stops just short.*

MARY: Amelia, come on now, it's time to go home. Daddy's waiting, and Lem.

AMELIA: I can't, Mamma...I'm afraid.

MARY: Afraid of what, Amelia? Everyone's been waiting for you for such a long time.

AMELIA: But mamma, I don't know how.

MARY: Amelia, baby, I'll show you. I know the way.

> *SAM crosses to AMELIA, carrying the dove from before. They are in both time periods at once. SAM and AMELIA the dove and make ready to realease him.*

SAM: Amelia. It's time.

AMELIA: No.

SAM: You promised. Remember? You said when it was time, we'd let him go. (Is he talking about the dove or SHAW?)

AMELIA: I know, but...

SAM: You promised. You have to have faith. Here. Take him. You saved him, you let him go.

AMELIA: I can't.

SAM: You can. Go ahead.

> *AMELIA releases the dove. SAM turns back to watch the dove as it wings its way home.*

AMELIA: Mamma? I'm so sorry, Mamma. I didn't mean what I said.

MARY: I know, sweetie, I know.

AMELIA: You don't hate me?

MARY: Oh, Amelia. No. Come oh, baby. It's time to go home.

AMELIA: I didn't get to...Oh Mamma.

MARY: What, sweetie?

AMELIA: It meant nothing. My life. It mean nothing.

MARY: It meant so much, Amelia. You don't know, do you? Your life saved so many others. Our pain came to something in the end, Amelia. It freed so many others, and that's as much as anyone can ask of their life. It's time.

> *AMELIA turns, tentatively at first, and run's into MARY'S deep embrace.*

AMELIA: I love you, Mamma.

> *LEM and JOHN join MARY and AMELIA. There is a loving reunion. JOHN and LEM hug AMELIA. JOHN kisses MARY. GOD has forgiven him and vice versa.*

> *Simultaneously, NADINE has been collecting things from MARY'S room. She straightens the bed.*

> *On the other side of the stage, SHAW has re-entered as his younger self. SAM has seen him and they share an embrace.*

> *The CHORUS watches as AMELIA and SHAW meet CS. AMELIA spits in her hand, SHAW looks at it unsure what to do. AMELIA keeps her hand held out, SHAW spits in his hand and shakes AMELIA's.*

The Girl In The White Pinafore

NADINE finishes making MARY'S bed. She places AMELIA'S picture on the pillow and drapes one red ribbon across it.

NADINE begins to exit, turns back.

NADINE: I love you, Mamma.

NADINE turns off the floor lamp and exits as the "Gracious Spirit" swells and the lights fade to black...

END OF PLAY

A NOTE

Because it is impossible to tell the individual stories of the approximately 312 souls taken in the New London explosion (accounts vary and we'll never really know), I have tried to channel the stories of many into one cohesive story. I did my best to stick to facts when it came to the causes of the explosion. However, other than the actual historic figure of W.C.Shaw, these characters are amalgams of many many different people. And, even though I have pulled from transcripts for the tribunal scenes, the named historical figures are not meant to portray those characters with 100% accuracy. Mr. Shaw especially is meant to be the study of a man caught in his own sorrow, guilt, and on his last day, dementia.

I am not seeking to make Shaw into either a villain or a martyr. My intent is to ask one question of him-- What is it like to have such a tragedy weighing on you in the last years of your life?

Just as I beg you not to make Shaw a monster just because it's the easy thing to do, I ask that both directors and actors be careful not to make Amelia some simple evil spirit. Or, worse, just angry to be angry. She is anything but. Do the work and suss out her motivations for not moving on. She is the very definition of a lost, hurt, and confused soul. And, so, is much more complex than one might initially think. She yearns for her mother's love and forgiveness at the same time she wants Shaw'a apology. She discovers apologies are hollow if you yourself cannot let go, but a mother's love can save. It's a hard line to walk-- strength and vulnerability. Your audience needs to connect with her struggle just as much as they connect with Shaw. We must see her arc.

Be careful of the easy way out on anything. It'd be easy to use blackouts between scenes. Truth be told, the scenes are divided the way they are simply to make it easy for me to toggle between or for you, as a director, to work with if doing a "scenes from" due to time constraints. (Educational theater competitors only.) Transitions should allow for the scenes to bleed into each other. It's why the Chorus is set up the way it is. Use "Old Man Shaw" for those transitions. You have my permission to throw it in where you need it-- transitions, underneath, intertwined. Be creative. Don't make it the whole show, but be creative.

My only intent here is to tell a story in a way that informs, entertains, and touches the actors telling the story and the audiences watching it. I'll leave it to you to decide if I succeeded. May we all find our own peace when the time comes.

Jiggs Burgess 03/02/2018

OLD MAN SHAW

Mary Mary
Jack and Jill
How many children
Did it kill...

Mattie, Mattie
Sim and Will
Count the graves
Upon the hill...

Billy Billy
Jim and Fred
How many babies
Cried and bled...

Willy, Willy
Sue and Ned
Heard his son
Lost his head...

Margy, Margy
Ruth and Belle
Do you hear a
Deathly knell...

Bobby, Bobby
June and Kel
Tears like rain
Flowed and fell...

COME, GRACIOUS SPIRIT, HEAV'NLY DOVE

Come, Gracious Spirit, heav'nly Dove,
with light and comfort from above;
be thou our guardian, thou our guide
o'er every thought and step preside,
o'er every thought and step preside.

The light of truth to us display,
and make us know and choose thy way;
plant holy fear in every heart,
that we from God may ne'er depart,
that we from God may ne'er depart.

Lead us to holiness, the road,
which we must take to dwell
with God lead us to Christ, the living way,
nor let us from his pastures stray,
nor let us from his pastures stray.

Lead us to God, our final rest,
to be with him forever blest
lead us to heav'n,
it's bliss to share fullness of joy, forever there,
fullness of joy, forever there.

COMPLETE TRANSCRIPT-- CAROLYN JONES (AGE 9) MARCH 25 1937 TO TEXAS LEGISLATURE

"Mr. President, members of the house of representatives, and friends of school children, I'm here today as a representative of the London school and as a survivor of the school explosion that took the lives of nearly 500 pupils, teachers, and parents. Last Thursday afternoon while my colleague and I were studying spelling for the interscholastic meet in which we were going to represent our school the next day, our teacher Mrs. Sory saw some pictures fall from the wall and several vases crash from the desk. In an instant she had jerked open two nearby windows and said get out of here. We were clinging to her when we heard the first awful rumble that in a few seconds caused the room to collapse. Mrs. Sory helped us out of the window and in another few seconds we were separated by the dark cloud of dust that blinded us. When it got so I could see again I ran home as fast as I could. My teacher and friend were not killed, but I did not see them again.

My sister Helen Jones, an honor student and member of the high school champion debate team, was not so fortunate. She and my uncle, Paul Grier, a senior who planned to study medicine, were both taken from us in this awful explosion that killed so many of the future generation of East Texas.

When the announcement was made a few hours earlier by our principle that school would be dismissed for the county meet, the usual joy and excitement of a holiday prevailed. Little did we realize that we soon would be searching in the ruins of our beautiful school building for the bodies of our sisters and brothers and teachers.

First, as a representative of these school friends and teachers of mine, both living and dead, I am here today to express our appreciation for all that you and our governor have done for the relief of the suffering people of this community. Second, let us suggest the legislature of Texas set aside a special day each year to be observed as a memorial day on which tribute will be paid to the children and teachers who died in this catastrophe. We want to thank you for the memorial fund to which many of you have already contributed and which people all over the world are sending donations. We believe if those students and teachers who died would speak they would want a living memorial instead of a stately building. By all means, we should have an appropriate but simple structure on which will appear the names of each pupil, teacher, and parent who died. With the remaining portion of money, our teachers suggest an endowment fund, to be used for the future education for the surviving children so that each might be assured of a college education if they so desired.

In conclusion, let me urge you, our lawmaking body, to make laws of safety, so it will not be possible for another explosion of this type to occur in the history of Texas schools. Our daddies and mothers, as well as the teachers, want to know that when we leave our homes in the morning to go to school, that we will come out safe when our lessons are over. Out of this explosion, we have learned of a new hazard that hovers about some of our school buildings. If this hazard can be forever blotted out of existence then we will not have completely lost our loved ones in vain. We need say nothing more on the point of safety legislation because we as children of London school know that our faith in our government will not be betrayed. We will have safe school buildings in the future. All of us who were spared will try to show our appreciation by striving to become the finest of citizens to carry on the work of this wonderful land of yours and mine. This is our plea, thank you."

... As a result of the New London tragedy, the 45th Legislature enacted House Bill 1017 which amended Article 6053, Texas Revised Civil Statutes, 1925, giving the Railroad Commission the authority to adopt rules and regulations pertaining to the odorization of natural gas or liquefied petroleum gases. On July 27, 1937, Gas Utilities Docket 122 was adopted and the Commission began enforcement of odorization requirements for natural gas.

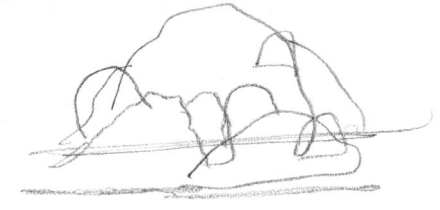

1st full run through: Mon 1/20

Sat. rehearsals 10-3pm

hazer/foggers?
rubble pile... smoker

Made in the USA
San Bernardino, CA
11 December 2019